Successful Self-Watering Containers:

Converting Your Favorite Container to a Self-Waterer

Lorraine Ballato

ISBN-13: 978-0-9820394-0-3
ISBN 10: 0-98203944-0-9

Designer: Stephen Roth

All photographs by Lorraine Ballato

To my husband Anthony who for over 30 years has been the rock upon whom I've built just about everything, not the least of which is this self watering container design.

Contents

Introduction

This is a short read. I would suggest that you take the time to go through the entire book, noting the photos and the Frequently Asked Questions (FAQs) before taking any action. You'll learn that you'll have options for your conversion, so buying supplies might turn out to be totally unnecessary. Plus you might want to organize a few friends to join you for a mini-workshop where you can share some purchases and split the costs, further minimizing any expense you may incur. That way, you can also share tools and techniques, especially if one of you is a fledgling do-it-yourselfer, the target audience for this book.

Keep in mind that this is meant to be a simple process, so don't make it more complicated than it needs to be. Because most of the material will be hidden from view when you are finished, you won't need to be too concerned about looks, such as uneven edges of internal liners. Not that I'm fostering poor workmanship, but I'm simply reminding you that some things don't need to be perfect, unless that's your particular preference.

You will, however, always need to be concerned about how it all works. So things such as water tightness and water seepage at the right point will be critically important, and you will need to test for that along the way.

So grab a cup of coffee or your preferred beverage, and settle down for a bit of light reading.

What Is a Self-Watering Container?

Actually, there is no such thing as a self-watering container. Just as a self-addressed envelope doesn't address itself (someone pre-addresses it), a container does not water itself. Someone actually needs to put water in it at some point.

A container is described as a self-watering container when it has a reservoir of water—and ideally, fertilizer—that a plant can access whenever it needs either or both. Once the initial setup is complete, the gardener need only "top off" the reservoir from time to time rather than water daily (or even more frequently depending on the plant and the conditions). The constant dependence of plant on gardener is lessened, as is the burden on the gardener to always provide water and nutrients on a timely basis to containerized plants. A self-watering container provides water and nutrients 24/7, and therein lies the difference between this system and any other watering and fertilizing system available.

Self-Watering Containers Not a New Idea

Self-watering containers have been around a lot longer than you might think. As far back as 1895, someone had already been working on devising a system to deliver water and nutrients to a containerized plant. A search through the United States Patent Office revealed more than a dozen patents in the United States alone on this one invention. Several of these patents even referred to work done outside the United States on the same concept.

Why so many, you might ask? That same thought occurred to me as well, so I spent some time examining those patent abstracts and drawings. A common issue seemed to be the size of the chambers that held the soil or the water—either or both were often disproportionately small, making it difficult to sustain the plant. Sometimes the water reservoir was so small, that it looked as if you might have to water more than twice a day with the system. What would be the point of that?

Some models had wicking systems. Others had variations in the way the water got into the reservoir. And on it went.

The Case for Self-Waterers or Who Cares Anyway?

Like you, I had been hearing and reading about self-watering containers, but I was happy with the containers I had. I knew of no other gardeners with self-waterers, and we all seemed resigned to the daily rituals of frequent watering and regular fertilizing that these decorative accents demanded. We would manage to find someone to water for us when we vacationed. We would learn techniques to provide slow and steady water—drip irrigation systems for containers. We would put some plants in water filled tubs. We would pray for rain. Along the way, some plants made it, and others did not. Fortunately, the stakes weren't and still aren't very high. But once you've experienced the extreme satisfaction of knowing that what you did helped an otherwise average plant to grow and thrive, transforming itself into stunning, lush vitality beyond your wildest imagination, I assure you that you ***will*** care.

I was fortunate to be asked to trial both The GardenPatch® Grow Box® and EarthBox® self-watering containers at the same time that I had to leave my raised vegetable bed fallow for a few seasons to rid it of some pathogens and squash borers. In the summer of 2007, I planted one with basil (that I have been growing for over thirty-five years), and tomatoes. I mixed granular fertilizer into the soil.

As long as I was at it, I figured I might as well trial more than just my vegetables this way. None of the local garden centers carried decorative containers that were self-waterers. Mail order vendors had interesting-looking self-waterers, but that expense would start to add up. One alternative was to get a mail order product to convert my containers to self-waterers, but this wouldn't fit all the sizes I had, and would cost a bundle when all was said and done. I did, however, order and use two of these conversion kits to test their usefulness. If they met my expectations, I reasoned, I could hope for an end-of-season sale to possibly stock up.

The self-watering container experiment resulted in one of the biggest discoveries in my gardening experience. What a revelation! The basil grew quickly and within eight weeks, I had plants that were more than thirty inches tall and wide with strong, woody trunks. I had never grown this healthy a basil plant so early in the season using a fertilized, raised bed with a soaker hose, which had been my old method. The tomatoes were also wildly successful—much better than what I had grown for the past fifteen years. Plants remained healthy and disease free; fruits were larger, tastier, and more plentiful right through October.

Best of all, I did not need to water these vegetable containers daily. With the exception of some ninety degree days, I was able to space my watering to three-day intervals as the plant roots reached into the reservoir for their needed water. What could be easier?

But the best experience of all was growing my beloved Angel's Trumpet (Brugmansia). **PHOTO 1** Who can resist that plant in full bloom with its huge, pendulous flowers gracefully perfuming the night air beneath a bedroom window, or on a patio? Anyone who grows this plant knows what a water hog it is. And getting it

PHOTO 1

to bloom on a regular basis takes so much fertilizer that you want to buy stock in the fertilizer company. The plant (purchased at an end of season sale for one dollar) got repotted into a container that was converted into a self-waterer. This time, the fertilizer was liquid and was delivered via the water reservoir, and the "top-off" occurred twice a week instead of twice a day.

That plant flushed four times with over twenty flowers each time in the course of a sixteen-week season. When it came into the basement for its winter rest (I think I heard it say, "Thank Heavens!"), it was still blooming, despite its bare branches and having fertilizer withheld from late August onward.

I was hooked— self-waterers were the way to go! Now I had the winter to figure out how to do that for the coming season without taking out a second mortgage on the house.

The Options for Self-Watering Containers

There's never been a better time for this product. Our busy lives are getting more demanding. Garden industry reports indicate that more people are growing more of their own food. This is being partly attributed to current economic conditions and also to concerns about quality. At Burpee alone, their CEO, George Ball, stated on National Public Radio's Science Friday, which took place on July 11, 2008, that growth in vegetable and herb sales had doubled. Furthermore, container gardening is currently one of the greatest growth areas in home gardening. If there were ever a time to think about converting to self-watering containers, it is now!

This hasn't gone unnoticed. A Google search for vendors of self-watering containers delivers no less than three main brands being sold by dozens of retail and mail-order companies. You'll also find some rather crude home-made do-it-yourself versions that may be very functional, but ugly does not even come close to describing their looks.

If you want to get new containers that are self-waterers, simply go to those vendors and make your purchases accordingly. On the other hand, if you have some of your own containers that you want to convert, or if you want to spend a lot less money and are somewhat handy, then the next few pages will be of great interest to you. Keep in mind—this is all about having bigger, more robust flowers, tastier vegetables, and overall healthier plants than you ever had in containers that weren't self-waterers.

My Do-It-Yourself Conversion Process will show you how to make your current round containers into self-waterers with a few things you should have around the house, and some relatively inexpensive purchases you can make locally or online. You don't have to be a master carpenter, or a have a set of power tools, or know advanced woodworking techniques to do this. But you do have to be able to handle simple do-it-yourself projects and follow simple instructions, which I'll lay out for you with some photos to help you along the way.

A Better Way: Converting Your Own Container

The recipe for a healthy containerized plant is: water, oxygen, light, and food. You must provide all of these in the proper amounts for a particular plant to survive. When you get it right, it thrives. Just tour a commercial greenhouse or ask any professional grower. For the rest of us, no matter what you think, data suggests that watering and fertilizing plants on a regular basis rarely delivers ideal amounts of food and water at just the right time.

In a self-watering container, a plant has the perfect amount of fertilizer (as much as it wants, as it's already there for the taking) and water (as much as it needs, as long as you keep the reservoir filled), oxygen, and light (You need to do that part correctly). Your steps to establishing this new system will be to create the water reservoir and a way to fill it, ensure oxygen can get to the roots of the plant, and determine when the reservoir needs to be refilled, all without spending a lot of money. Fertilizer is a variable that will be different depending on what's in the container.

WHAT YOU NEED:

To start, have a pencil and paper handy, as well as a ruler or tape measure.

To create the water reservoir, first you need to have a shelf inside the container for the plant and potting medium to rest on. That is a product you will need to buy either at your local garden center or online.

You then need to measure your container. Measure across the top of the pot on the inside, and do the same across the bottom of the pot. Add the two numbers together and divide that number by two. You should get a number such as eight or

PHOTO 2

PHOTO 3

ten. Write that number down. That's the diameter of the insert you will need to purchase. There are two products on the market. One is called Ups-A-Daisy® (Daisy), and is a bright orange, hard plastic, perforated disk with two large holes in it. **PHOTO 2** It comes in diameters ranging from ten inches through eighteen inches, and can cost anywhere from about five dollars to thirteen dollars, depending on size. You can get them at independent garden centers and online. The other is called AirBase®. It is also circular and perforated, but without larger holes. **PHOTO 3** It comes in diameters ranging from four to ten inches and is priced from about three dollars to fourteen dollars, depending on the size and quantity. I've only seen it available from mail-order and online vendors.

If your pot is sized such that you need an AirBase®, immediately stop, and go to the References section of this book on page 55 to order the correct size of insert from the vendor of your choice.

Next you need to make the water reservoir. This must be a watertight chamber that will endure for the entire season and hopefully longer than that, so you don't have to re-do this next year. You can make this using pond liner (my personal favorite), which is available at garden centers, pond supply stores, some hardware stores, and some home improvement stores. **PHOTO 4** You can also use four or six-millimeter thick plastic sold in hardware and home improvement centers as drop cloths for painting. These are a little harder to work with, but when they are doubled up, they do the job. Shower curtains and shower curtain liners are also quite functional.

Your third component is the fill tube, needed to deliver the

PHOTO 4

PHOTO 5

water to the reservoir. This is PVC pipe, although I prefer to use electrical conduit. Both come in the same size and have the same markings: ¾" PVC40, which is sold in ten-foot lengths. It has an outside diameter of 13/16" and an inside diameter of 5/8". **PHOTO 5** The advantage of the electrical conduit is that it is gray instead of the stark white of PVC, which will be harder to camouflage when the container is planted. While you're at the hardware store, get a package of #18 O-Rings **PHOTO 6**, which you'll also need for the fill tube.

For your water level indicator—to tell you when you need to top

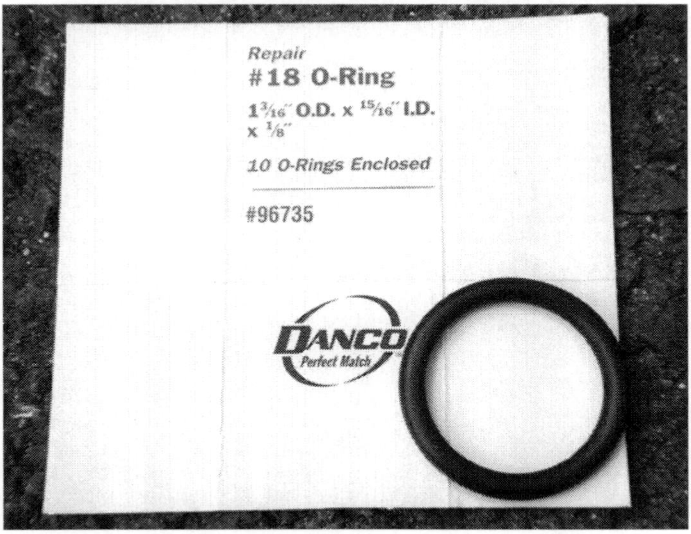

PHOTO 6

off your reservoir—you have a couple of options. Scout around the house to see what you can find. Look for corks, foam rubber, Styrofoam (not the beads or peanuts), drinking straws that are about twelve inches in length, and twelve-inch long wooden skewers that are usually used for grilling food. Any of these can be worked into this. For very large containers, I was able to find a three-foot length of 1/8″ wooden dowel in my local crafts store for twenty-nine cents. **PHOTO 7**

The key here is to use components that will float and that

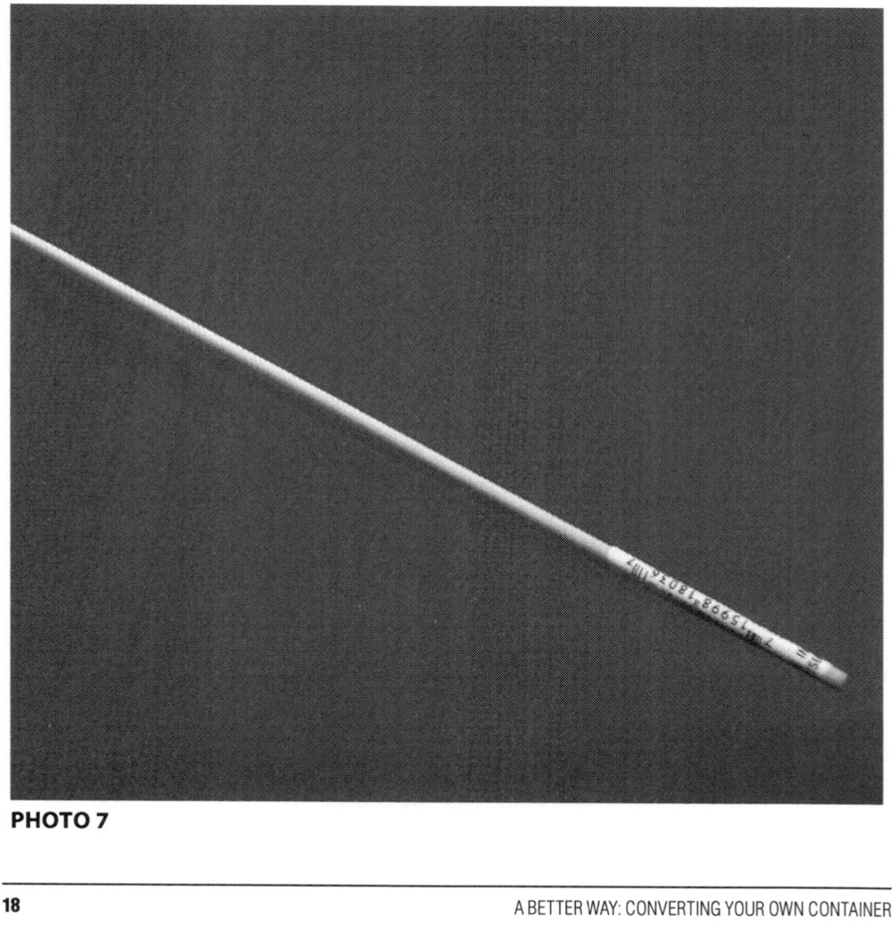

PHOTO 7

are waterproof, including waterproof caulking compound or waterproof glue that is acid-free to hold these pieces together when it's time to assemble them. Whatever you don't have, you can buy at a craft store for virtually pennies to a few dollars.

The rest of your supplies are all items an average do-it-yourselfer should have readily available. All you need to do is gather them up. Whatever you don't have, use that paper and pencil to start a list, but hold back from running out to purchase anything until you've gotten to the end of this book.

Complete Supply List

- Awl
- Caulking Compound or Glue (waterproof)
- Container Insert, properly sized for your container:
  either AirBase® Insert for reservoirs four to ten inches in diameter or Ups-A-Daisy® Insert for reservoirs ten inches in diameter and larger
- Cork (plastic or natural) **PHOTO 8** (with skewers)
- Chalk (pastel colored or other light colored pen or pencil)
- Dowel (1/8″ wooden)
- Drill with a ¼″ Bit
  (possibly a second bit for use on ceramics or masonry)
- Drill Bit for AirBase® hole,
  (1¼″ [32 mm] for use on plastic for small pots) **PHOTO 9**
- Foam Rubber
- Hair Dryer
- Marking Pen (waterproof, such as a Sharpie®)
- Masking Tape
- Nail Polish or Paint (orange or red)
- O-Rings (#18)
- Pond Liner, Plastic Shower Curtain, or Plastic Drop Cloth
- PVC or Electrical Conduit
  (3/4″ PVC 40, outside diameter 13/16″, inside diameter 5/8″)

- Safety Glasses
- Sandpaper
- Saw (ordinary handsaw or keyhole saw—not a hacksaw)
- Scissors (very sharp)
- Skewers (bamboo or wooden dowel)
- Straws
- Styrofoam **PHOTO 10** (Package of 1″ Balls)
- Tape Measure or Ruler
- Utility Knife with a New Blade

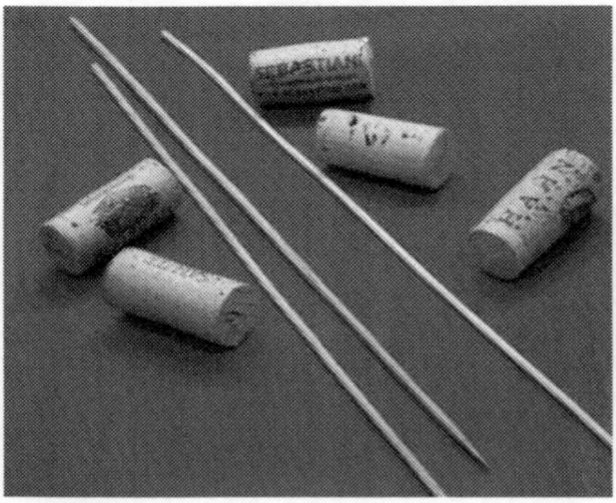

PHOTO 8

PHOTO 9

PHOTO 10

DirectRoot
AirBase®
Pot Drainag
Insert
Better than gravel!
Lighter and allows more room for roots to grow!
Prevents waterlogged soil
and root rot!
Keeps dirt in, lets excess water out!
Simply pick the AirBase that
most closely fits pot bottom
and repot as normal.
Perfect drainage
made EASY!
For best drainage, be sure pot has at
least one drainage hole. Can be used as
a drainage platform in pots with no
holes or as a self-watering reservoir.
Multi-Patented
Made in the USA
6.5AB

PHOTO 11

Putting It All Together: Building Your Self-Watering Container

PREPARING YOUR CONTAINER

If you're using an AirBase®, now is the time to make a hole in it so you will be able to work with the other components. Using the 1 ¼" drill bit, choose any second hole from the outside edge of the AirBase® and use it as your starter hole. Slowly engage the drill until the hole is drilled through. Remove the drill and the plastic you've just eliminated from the AirBase®. That plastic disk you just drilled out is trash. You now have a work hole which will later be the receptacle for your fill tube. **PHOTO 11**

If there is a hole in the bottom of your container, you are ready to go to the next step. If your container is a cachepot and has no drainage, you'll have to drill or puncture a hole to prevent excess water buildup. Rainstorms can cause the reservoir to overflow into the soil mix and waterlog the roots, depriving your plants of the necessary oxygen they'll need to survive, and all your work will be for naught.

This hole can be on the side below where the insert will sit, but that can sometimes be an eyesore, detracting from the beauty of the container. If you make the hole on the side, you must first place your insert inside, determine where in the container it will rest and place your weep hole approximately an inch below that level. If you're using a Daisy, you'll see that it has two large holes—one in the center and one toward the edge. These are called lift holes. You'll find out where to place your weep hole by inserting a ruler into either of the large holes in the Daisy and measuring the distance from the bottom of the Daisy to the bottom of the container. For the AirBase®, use the only large hole you have made to take this measurement. Write that number down. Remove the ruler and measure that same distance on the outside of the container. Although that's not the same distance from the bottom of the insert (you need to account for the width of the bottom layer of the container) you still subtract an inch from your measurement and make your hole at that distance from the bottom of the container. This will ensure that enough oxygen can get to the roots of your plants, even in an over-watering situation.

You can also place your weep hole on the bottom where container drainage holes are usually found. That would be my recommendation, as it will make it easier for you to catch overflow water if and when you bring this self-waterer into any living space. These containers are really very useful for more than just this outdoor/vacation/vegetable application.

A fiberglass or resin container is much easier to work with than ceramic or terra cotta. Lighter in weight and easier to drill, you can tailor your self-watering needs with fewer concerns about breakage and handling. When you drill this weep hole, start it first by using your awl from the outside. Make the hole by hand; don't use a hammer, as that would likely crack the pot. Use a small drill bit—certainly no larger than 1/4"—to further open and neaten the hole. Remember, it's a weep hole—not a full drainage hole.

If your pot is ceramic or terra cotta, the awl is unnecessary. Mark the spot on the container where you want to make the hole. Use a ceramic or masonry drill bit and surround the targeted area with masking tape to prevent potential shattering. Be sure to use eye protection as well. Engage the slow speed on the drill and be patient until the hole is completed. Use fine sandpaper with a gloved hand to smooth the edges of the new hole.

CREATING THE WATER RESERVOIR

Working with the pond liner or plastic is the most time consuming and hardest part of this process, because the material wants to dance with you. Before you get started working with it, it's best to get your masking tape all lined up in little strips so you can tame the liner/plastic as you go along. It's for this same reason I would strongly advise you to have your insert ready to go as well. It turns out to be a great holder once you have fit the liner into the container.

PHOTO 12

This resin container in **PHOTO 12** measured fourteen inches across the inside at the top and eight inches across the inside at the bottom. That totaled twenty-two inches. Half of twenty-two inches is eleven inches, which is the size of the Daisy used (AirBase® doesn't come larger than ten inches) for this container.

Note that both the Daisy and the AirBase® sit a bit higher in the container when the label is face down. That means you can get a slightly larger reservoir when you place it label side down. However, the manufacturer has taken great pains to create a beveled edge on the Daisy for stability and doesn't recommend that it be used upside down. Yet a larger water reservoir can be useful for thirsty plants like elephant ears, caladiums, and angel's trumpets, for example.

Start by placing your Daisy into your container as in **PHOTO 13** and measure the distance from the bottom of the Daisy to the bottom of your container. When the Daisy is inside this container, there is a space of 4 ½″ from the bottom of the Daisy to the bottom of the container. Write this number down.

Place your pond liner/plastic on a work table and place your insert on top of it. Using your Sharpie® for the plastic or the chalk/light colored pencil for the pond liner, mark an area that is two to three inches larger than the measurement of the distance from the bottom of the pot to the insert when inside the pot (the number you wrote down). Check your measurements before cutting. Keep in mind the famous quote from Norm Abram of This Old House fame, "measure twice; cut once." Once you're sure, use those sharp scissors to make this cut.

PHOTO 13

Place the cut liner/plastic over the container, making sure it's even all around the container. **PHOTO 14**

PHOTO 14

Slowly, with one hand, work it into the container until it rests on the bottom. **PHOTO 15**

Pleats will form on the side, and as they do, gently coax all of them to lay in the same direction. This will be important later on when you need to have your insert sit level and steady in your container.

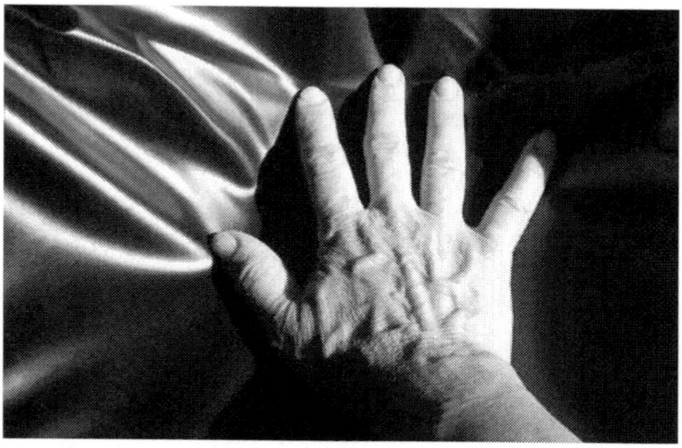

PHOTO 15

Have lots of masking tape lined up in little strips all around your pot as in **PHOTO 16** and use it freely to temporarily hold things in place. If it's cold, use the hair dryer to make the plastic/liner easier to work with.

PHOTO 16

Tape as much as you can as high as you can **PHOTO 17** so the taping will be above where the insert will rest. If you have some moisture inside the container, it will cut down on some of

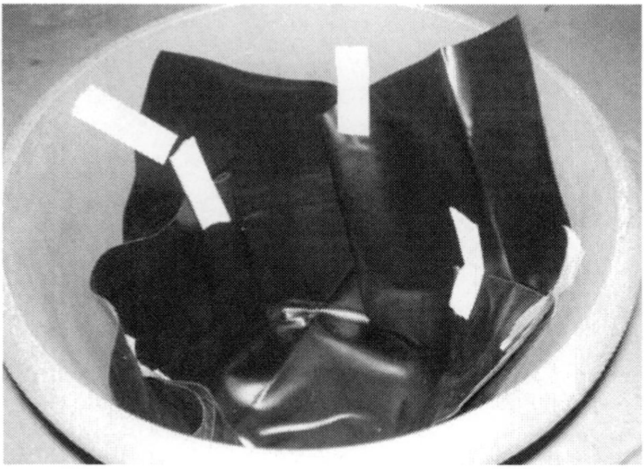

PHOTO 17

the slipping, but you want a little slipping to help with the final fitting. On the other hand, total dryness isn't the best condition either.

Once you have the liner settled in, tape it all around so it doesn't move on you.

Gently place the insert back inside, **PHOTO 18** being sure not to wedge it in just yet.

Using the right marking pen or pencil, draw a line inside the pot to indicate the top where the insert rests, and gently remove the insert.

If your pot drains from the bottom, you need to make a weep hole in the liner. At approximately two inches below the line

PHOTO 18

that you've drawn, pinch the liner and cut a hole the size of the head of a screwdriver. This is more than a puncture—you should actually remove a piece of the plastic or pond liner.

Replace the insert, not yet in its permanent position, and carefully fill the reservoir. You need to test that it holds water and also drains through the weep hole. Fill it above the top of the insert and watch it drain. It should stop draining once the water drops below the weep hole. If it continues to drain, you may have a leak somewhere that you need to find, or the liner may have slipped somehow. If that happened, the weep hole in the liner could have moved lower on the pot. Otherwise, you have successfully made your reservoir.

Next, dump your water out. You need to have an empty pot for the rest of the assembly.

Assuming this all worked, you can now "final fit" your reservoir. Gently remove your insert. Be sure the plastic/liner is taped and that the pleats are taped close to the line you made where the insert rests. Using that line as a guide, use your scissors to cut about an inch to two inches above it for the final fit of the plastic/liner. Be prepared to tape the plastic/liner to the pot again once the cut has been made. Later on, you'll need to keep the plastic/liner against the pot when you fill it with potting mix, and the tape will help you do that.

It will be very tempting to just take a utility knife to cut the plastic/liner while it rests against the container. I know because I was there and tried it. Let me tell you from experience, it's much harder and in the long run, it didn't work. But go ahead and try it if you're so inclined. Have a large supply of liner/plastic around for your second go at it.

Once the reservoir has been trimmed, you've finished the hardest part of this assembly. **PHOTO 19**

PHOTO 19

MAKING THE FILL TUBE

Now you're ready to make your fill tube, using the large hole in the insert on the edge (not the one in the center) of the Daisy. The outside holes in all of the Daisys are the same size regardless of the size of Daisy you use. Once you have your ten-foot length (that's how they're sold—it costs the grand sum of $1.19 for ten feet of PVC or electrical conduit), you're all set.

Using your tape measure, insert it into the hole and note the distance from the bottom of the container to the top of the pot. Write that number down. Measure that same distance on the PVC itself and use your Sharpie® to mark the length. Measure twice; cut once. Using your keyhole or handsaw, cut your PVC to that length. Do not use power tools to cut your PVC. That would shatter it, making it very dangerous. Do not use a hacksaw—the teeth are too fine for the plastic piping and will only make a mess of the tool. Once the PVC has been cut, carefully take off the rough edges by scraping them with a utility knife and a gloved hand.

Gently insert the pipe into the lift hole so that the bottom of the pipe rests on the bottom of the reservoir. **PHOTO 20**

PHOTO 20

PHOTO 21

Take one #18 O-ring and gently roll it onto the pipe **PHOTO 21** so that it rests at the juncture of the pipe and the insert. **PHOTO 22**

PHOTO 22

Slowly lift the pipe off the floor of the reservoir so that the O-ring is about ¾" above the insert. Hold it there and gently roll the O-ring further down the pipe so that it is once again at the juncture of the pipe and the insert. You can let go now since the O-ring is holding the fill tube off the floor of the reservoir, which will help the water flow easier and faster into the chamber. It will also prevent the fill tube from chafing the reservoir and wearing a hole in the liner.

Turn the fill tube to be sure any printing on the pipe faces the inside of the container so when the plants are in place, it will be easier to camouflage the fill tube.

BUILDING THE WATER LEVEL INDICATOR (WLI)

How will you know when it's time to top off the reservoir? You can either do this on a schedule, but that doesn't always work. Who can predict weather, personal emergencies, and the like? Or you can refill the self-waterer when you pass by with a hose, but that kind of defeats the purpose of the whole thing, wouldn't you say?

And how much water should you put in? Well, you could just fill it up until it comes out the weep hole, but that's kind of wasteful and the downstairs neighbor doesn't always like it when you rain on her balcony, and besides, the fertilizer in the water just gets washed away, and, and, and....

How about something that tells you when it's time to fill 'er up? Enter the water level indicator (WLI).

With your fill tube in place, you can make your WLI—and it can actually be fun. It has to have three qualities: it needs to be a little longer than the length of your fill tube; it needs to be able to float; and it needs to be both noticeable and inconspicuous at the same time among the plants in the container.

To fit into the fill tube, you get to carve your chosen material to just shy of the width of the PVC. Your float can be made from foam rubber, Styrofoam (avoid peanuts and beads, which are manufactured with dimples that make it nearly impossible to get a good fit), or cork. My preferred float material is cork— both the natural as well as the plastic composite work fine. So first you have to invite some friends over to share a bottle of wine. Or make some new friends from whom you can get their corks. Or maybe your local wine store does wine tastings and they wouldn't mind giving you a few of their old corks.

Then take that cork from the bottle and carve it so it fits freely into the fill tube. Using those sharp scissors, simply cut the cork in half, cut those sharp edges off, and you now have two floats for water level indicators as shown in **PHOTO 23**. Be mindful that the cork will absorb some water during the course of the season so be extra certain that you cut it to allow for slight expansion and still float freely.

If you don't have any of the float materials, try your local craft store. Mine had a dozen one-inch Styrofoam balls, which I easily shaped with those same scissors. **PHOTO 24**

Once you've done that, measure a drinking straw or a wooden

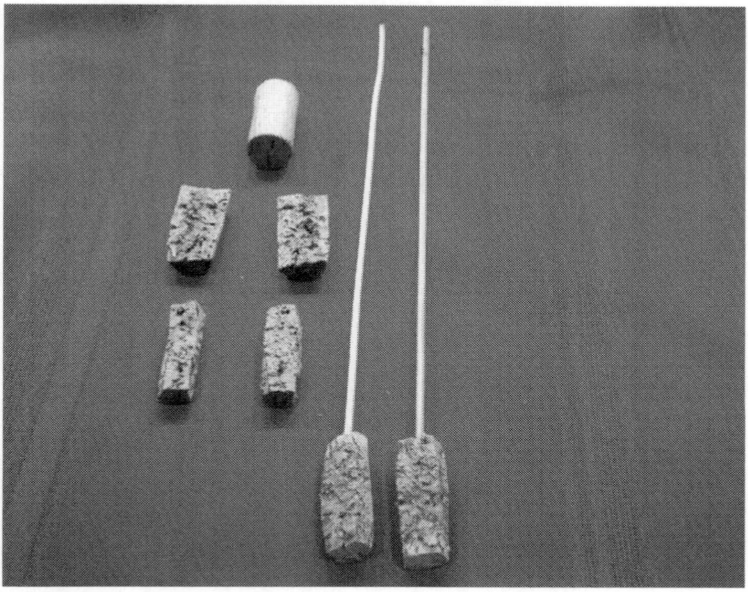

PHOTO 23

PHOTO 24

skewer cut a little bit longer than the length of the fill tube (you can always cut more off later if you don't want that much showing). One of my containers was taller than the skewer, so again, my local crafts store came to the rescue. They had a thirty-six inch length of 1/8" wooden dowel for twenty-nine cents. Worked for me.

A few inches at the tip of the skewer/straw/dowel will need to be painted a bright, noticeable color. Nail polish works great or you can use an indelible, waterproof marking pen.

If you're using a straw or dowel, you need to use your awl to make a hole in the center of the cork/Styrofoam large enough to accept it. Be aware that cork flakes, so you'll have to be patient and go slowly. It's a small piece that could easily fall apart. If you're using a skewer, simply use the pointed end as shown in **PHOTO 25** to make the hole you need.

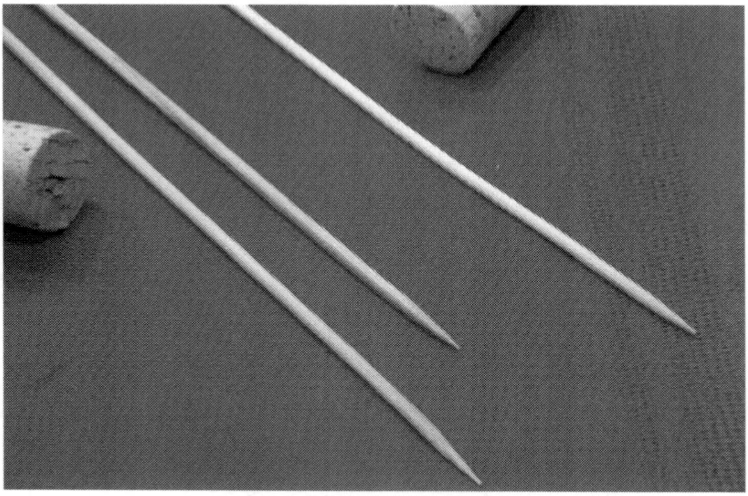

PHOTO 25

PHOTO 26

Once you've made the hole, apply the glue per the directions on the label to secure the straw/dowel/skewer.

When it's cured, place it in the fill tube. Your WLI will be its least visible when the reservoir is lowest as seen in **PHOTO 26**. The more of it you see, the more water is in the reservoir. **PHOTO 27** Each container and reservoir will be different and you will learn to "read" each one. Once your WLI is out of sight, that means your reservoir is running low or is empty—not a good thing for your plants.

PHOTO 27

Decide on the length you want and cut your indicator to fit using the scissors. Place it in the fill tube and decide whether you want to leave it "au natural" so it blends in better with the plants or not. That's my preference. Test its visibility by filling the reservoir and noting your "flag." When you've got this the way you want it, dump the water out.

THE FINAL FIT: SETTING UP YOUR SELF-WATERING CONTAINER

Now you can complete your newly converted self-watering container.

Considering what you've accomplished and the notion that you might want to convert more planters, taking some notes at this point might not be a bad idea. For example, what size of insert did you use? Was your original working piece for the reservoir about two feet by two feet or did it need to be larger?

Up to now, your insert has been in place in a somewhat loose fashion. Go ahead and remove the label, making certain the insert is level and that your liner is positioned properly.

Keep the liner taped to the edges so when you fill the pot with potting mix, as little as possible gets between the liner and container.

If you made your weep hole on the side of your container, place your fill tube on the same side of the container so you can see when the water is running out of it if necessary.

I have found it helpful to angle the fill tube slightly outward to facilitate fill ups. **PHOTO 28**

Once you think you have everything placed the way you need to, go ahead and gently but firmly wedge the insert into place.

That's it. Now you're ready for your plants to live in this new world. Set your container up in your favorite workspace, but don't fill the reservoir until you have it where it will finally rest. That water weight will make it much heavier than it would be otherwise. It's better to fill it up after you've got it in place. Also, this system doesn't negate the need for pot feet, so get them lined up as well before you move your container to its designated spot in the garden.

Once you have your plants in the self-watering container, water them from the top until they "root in." Let the reservoir fill as the water drains from the soil above it for the first two weeks or so until the plants start to reach down. You'll be able to tell right away when this happens. Make sure the reservoir is filled to capacity, even to the point of overflow through your weep holes. You want your plants to get the idea that water is waiting for them whenever they want it, just inches away. Stretch the length of time between your watering after the first week to encourage them to reach. They will find their water supply and really take off.

You'll get so much more than time out of this system; you'll wonder why it's been such a sleeper.

PHOTO 28

FAQs

How do I fertilize my plants in self-watering containers?

You can mix water soluble fertilizer into your planting mix and you can also mix liquid fertilizer into the water reservoir.

I'm worried that potting soil might get into the water reservoir through the holes in the inserts. How can I prevent that?

Keep the liners taped to the sides when you fill the containers. Don't worry about dirt going into the water reservoir. A little might get in, but if it bothers you, place a single sheet of newspaper there (not the shiny pages) which will decompose quickly.

Newspaper is printed on biodegradable paper with soy based inks and has proven to be an excellent and safe compostable material as long as you use only the non-shiny pages. Over the course of a season, it will break down while still allowing water and nutrients to pass through. It's a great weed suppressor and is being used throughout the world as a base for garden mulch and in compost piles, eliminating millions of pounds of refuse and trash.

The reservoir will take up the space I think my plant needs for roots. How can I be sure my plant has enough "root room?"

The roots reach into the reservoir, so they actually go beyond that "top shelf" the insert creates. Additionally, you can change the sizes of the top and bottom parts of the container by simply using bigger or smaller inserts that will still fit the container. It's especially helpful to do this if you know you have a very thirsty plant that demands inordinate amounts of water, such as a Brugmansia. As another alternative, you can always go to a bigger container, which in the case of a Brugmansia is usually inevitable.

How does oxygen get to the plant?

The perforations in the inserts are enough to provide the necessary oxygen as long as the weep hole you make in the reservoir is at least an inch below the insert. As the plant drinks the water, more oxygen is allocated to the plant until the next water refill.

Can I use the straw from a broken bottle of Fantastic® or some other sprayer that has broken?

Yes, as long as you have thoroughly washed it with hot soapy water. The straw from a spray bottle is very rigid and does a fine job once it's attached to your float and painted.

Can I use trash bags for the liners to make my reservoir?

You may be tempted to use trash bags. Don't! They are so slippery, it will take you about two minutes of "arguing" with one of those trash bags to convince you to abandon that idea, no matter how committed you may be to its many uses in the home.

Can this system be used for hanging baskets?

Absolutely! It's one of the best things you can do for hanging baskets, as they have a tendency to dry out very quickly, especially if they are lined with coir. This is where the AirBase® inserts come in handy because they are sized on a smaller scale. You need to be concerned, however, about weight, as water can really be heavy. Be sure that whatever you are using to hold your hanging basket can indeed handle the water weight. The rule of thumb is that a pint (sixteen ounces) of water weighs about one pound so be aware of that.

Can I use Crazy Glue® to make my Water Level Indicator?

Do not try to use Crazy Glue®. It's caustic and will decompose the things you'll try to fuse except, of course, your fingers.

What are moisture crystals?

Moisture crystals are commercially available polymers which are formulated to absorb several times their weight in water. They are designed to be mixed into potting mixes, moistened, and then release that moisture back to the plants gradually between waterings.

Do you recommend using moisture crystals in self-watering containers?

I wouldn't recommend using moisture crystals until you have a little experience with specific plants and specific situations. You can always add them later but it's nearly impossible to remove them.

Rather than creating an entire reservoir, wouldn't it be easier to just patch the drainage holes with some kind of waterproof cement and go from there?

That was the first idea I tried and I am sorry to say that I couldn't manage to get a watertight seal that held up for an indefinite period of time. Just like garden hose connections, they eventually all leaked, defeating the purpose.

One Last Story

If after reading through this, you have any reservations about using this system, let me share one last experience.

We recently removed two ailing maple trees from the front of the house, and in doing so, when I or anyone else walks out my front door, we now have this wonderful view of our well head **PHOTO 29** which is in a fairly "hard to reach with a hose" place.

PHOTO 29

PHOTO 30

At about two feet tall, it takes a sizable planter to hide it and we need to be able to leave it accessible for repairs. (I try not to think about that. The well is four hundred feet deep!) What better place for a self-waterer? And of course, Kong coleus I thought would be the ideal plant for this shady nook.

I set up the planter with some elephant ears for interest **PHOTO 30**, hiding the fill tube within that mass of foliage.

In the "before" photo I think I caught the ducks trying to escape. **PHOTO 31**

PHOTO 31

But with the planter in place, I thought I heard them say they would stay a while longer.

The "after" photo was taken just four short weeks later. **PHOTO 32** The ducks have indeed stayed and the foliage has reached well into the canopy of the nearby Japanese maple, completely hiding the well head.

Upon closer inspection, **PHOTO 33** you can see the vitality of the plant, which has only been topped off once a week because it's in the shade. It has been fed through fertilizer mixed into the potting soil. What could be easier and a better seasonal solution?

PHOTO 32

PHOTO 33

REFERENCES

AirBase® available through Lee Valley Tools LTD., www.leevalley.com and www.directroot.com

EarthBox®, www.earthbox.com

Gardeners Supply, www.gardeners.com

Incredible Vegetables from Self-Watering Containers, Edward C. Smith, January, 2006, Storey Publishing.

Lechuza, www.lechuza.com

The GardenPatch® Grow Box®, www.agardenpatch.com

Ups-A-Daisy®, www.ups-a-daisy.com

INDEX

Bold page numbers indicate photograph.

NOTES